ARRANGING
FOR HORNS
JERRY GATES

To access audio visit:
www.halleonard.com/mylibrary
Enter Code
5689-4396-3340-9785

ACKNOWLEDGMENTS

This could not have been written without the help of many fine people. A big thank you goes to past teachers Jack Smalley, Dick Grove, and Allyn Ferguson. They not only taught me music, but through their actions, about life and how it can be lived. A special thank you to Donny Nolan who, through his own love of music, helped me embrace the art form early on in my career.

A big thanks to Debbie Cavalier for her help in making this publication possible at Berklee Press and the fine editing of Jonathan Feist, whose guidance, expertise in the field, and common sense feedback cannot be measured.

Finally, a special thank you to my family—Lori, Vance, and Annette—for being on life's path with me. You make it all worthwhile.

INTRODUCTION

When I was a teenager, I never thought of becoming a writer of musical ideas. I just wanted to be a rock star, like bassist John Entwistle of the Who. That all changed once I was exposed to horn bands and various ensembles, after high school. It was intriguing to me that an instrumentalist could not only bring the notes I wrote to life, in a sense, but could add his or her own personality and interpretation of those notes. Better yet, the audience clapped if they liked what I had written! Since those early days of my career, I've written for ensembles of all shapes and sizes including the orchestra. In this book, I will share some of the many things, specifically about horn writing, that I've learned along the way.

If you are looking for a book to lead you through techniques and craft of arranging for horn sections, this is it. *Arranging for Horns* is a guide that will take you from the fundamental ranges and transpositions of the most common horns used in popular music today to sophisticated, time tested voicings that will let you create both simple and complex sounds. I've distilled what are sometimes presented as complex ideas down to simple, practical concepts. Additionally, I've presented two key arranging strategies—the role(s) or job an instrument can perform during an arrangement, and also an arrangement's contour/shape that can affect the audience. These two topics are often just as important to the final version of your arrangement as are the notes themselves.

ABOUT THE ACCOMPANYING AUDIO

To access the accompanying audio, go to www.halleonard.com/mylibrary and enter the code found on the first page of this book. This will grant you instant access to every example. Examples with accompanying audio are marked with an audio icon.

RHYTHM SECTION REVIEW

Before we get to the horns, let's review some notation practices regarding the rhythm section.

The rhythm section can consist of just drums, bass, and piano or guitar, but it can also get much larger, with the addition of multiple guitars, keyboards, percussionists, and others. Understanding how to write for the rhythm section players will allow you to include them more fully into your arrangements, as well as aiding in your study of scores.

The arrangements in the following chapters include a basic rhythm section: drum set, bass, piano, and guitar. We use the following standards for symbols and terminology, as we discuss their roles and functions.

Starting with the drum set, the primary roles for this instrument are to keep time, help articulate the style or "groove," and accent various rhythms that the writer deems important. Figure I.1 illustrates a typical rock or funk drum part in 3-part notation (bass drum, snare drum, cymbals).

FIG. I.1. Rock/Funk Drum in 3-Part Notation

The groove or pattern is established in the first two measures. Slashes, along with the word "simile," are used to indicate that the pattern continues "similarly to" the notated measures until something changes. In measure 9, the pattern changes, so the notation does as well. The word "fill" above measure 12 means that the player is to create a brief improvisation, outside the continuing pattern, to fill musical space within the arrangement. Tempo, style, and dynamic markings at bar 1 indicate additional information about the performance.

In measure 16 of figure I.1, rhythmic notation is used to tell the drummer what rhythm to play in that measure. This form of notation is often used when the complete ensemble has a rhythm to play as a unit or "tutti." These symbols can be used for the rest of the rhythm section as well. Figure I.2 shows each regular note value with its corresponding rhythmic notation symbol.

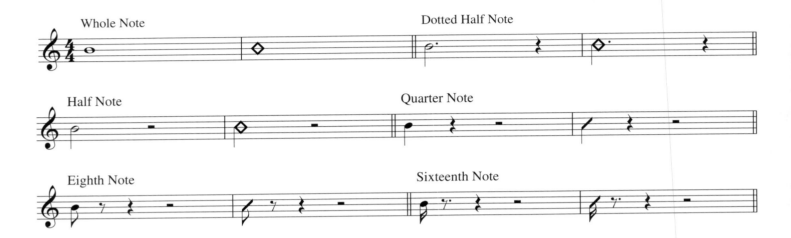

FIG. I.2. Rhythmic Notation Equivalents

In jazz, a simple but effective notation technique used is called "kicks over time." *Time* refers to the continuing groove, indicated by the slashes, and *kicks* refer to the accents notated on top of the staff that you want the player to perform. In figure I.3, the drummer is playing in a jazz or swing style, incorporating the rhythms indicated above the staff into the drum pattern, as appropriate.

FIG. I.3. Kicks Over Time

Electric and acoustic bass parts are often written using a combination of pitches, slashes, and rhythmic notation. Figure I.4 shows a combination of notation techniques. Note that this bass part is written for a 5-string instrument, which is able to play the written D below the bass clef. Bass notation sounds an octave lower than written.

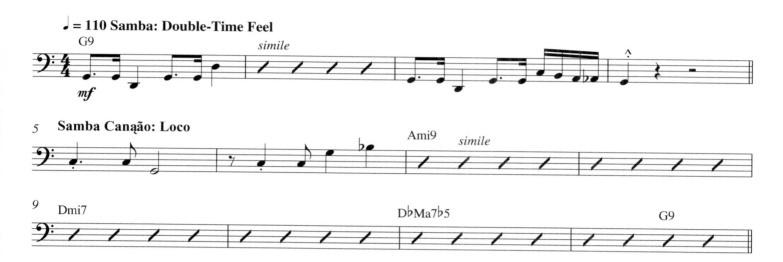

FIG. I.4. Samba Double-Time Feel

Similar to drum notation, once the pattern is established, slashes and the word "simile" can be used for bass parts or other instruments. However, unlike drum notation, chord symbols must be included above the slashes to indicate the harmonic source of the notes. This form of notation can be used in any rhythm-section based style.

A special note should be said about slash notation, rhythmic notation, and chord symbols: *Always keep in mind the player(s) that may be performing your music.* For example, many performers, especially those trained in traditional classical music, have not received instruction regarding how to read chord symbols or how to interpret the slashes. If you suspect that this will be the case, write out the part in standard notation. It takes a little more time to write the part, but it leaves less to the possibility that a player won't know how to interpret what you have written. Always use the notational technique that is best for the player, in order to get the best performance of your music.

Figure I.5 is an example of a typical guitar part. There are slashes, rhythmic notation, chord symbols, and specific pitches (written an octave higher than where they sound). These are the same techniques that are used to create bass parts. The style of the music, dynamic markings, and tempo are indicated as well. In this case, there is an assumption by the writer that the guitarist understands the styles of samba-canção (a slow samba from Brazil) and samba, and so will be able to add appropriate rhythms to the given chord symbols when slash notation is used. Note the added direction of "With Distortion" where the player is to use that electronic effect. Any information that will help the player understand exactly what you, the writer, would like the performer to do should be included in the notation.

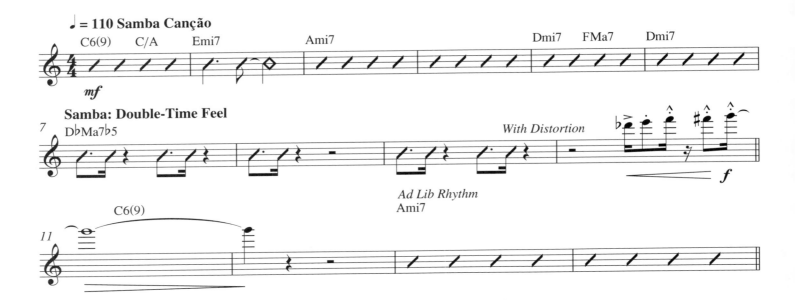

FIG. I.5. Samba Guitar Part

Piano notation styles can be quite varied—even within the same piece of music. In classical piano notation, all notes and rhythms are written out. However, once modern chord symbols and rhythmic notation were adopted to facilitate communication of musical ideas and give more freedom to interpret the music, piano parts became quite varied with the amount of information that needed to be written.

Figure I.6 illustrates the use of a grand staff. In this case, modern chord symbols by themselves will not convey the exact voicing and notes to be sounded, so all pitches and rhythms need to be written.

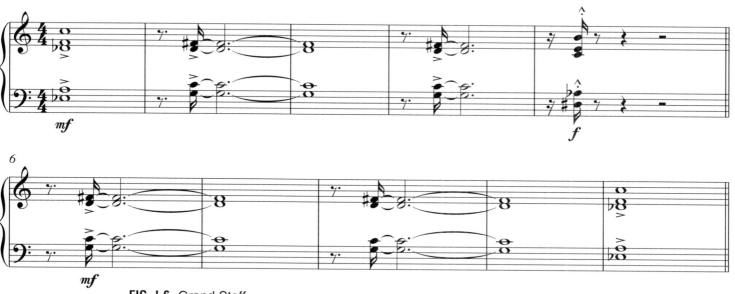

FIG. I.6. Grand Staff

Figure I.7, bar 1, represents another type of notation for piano. Here, the assumption is that the performer will interpret chord symbols to create the correct harmonic support for the melody. Not only is the tempo marked as "rubato" (i.e., flexible tempo), but the instruction is to "ad lib" the melody using the chord symbols as a guide. The performer will not only supply the correct harmony indicated by the chord symbols, but also has been given the license to interpret the melody based on his or her creative expression.

Innocent Wonder

FIG. I.7. "Innocent Wonder"

Figure I.8 illustrates yet another technique that can be used to convey musical information to the pianist. Here, slashes are used to tell the player that he should play harmony indicated by the chord symbols. What rhythms the player uses for that harmony is completely up to the performer and his or her understanding of the given style. Additionally, rhythmic notation and pitches are used where specific rhythms are needed.

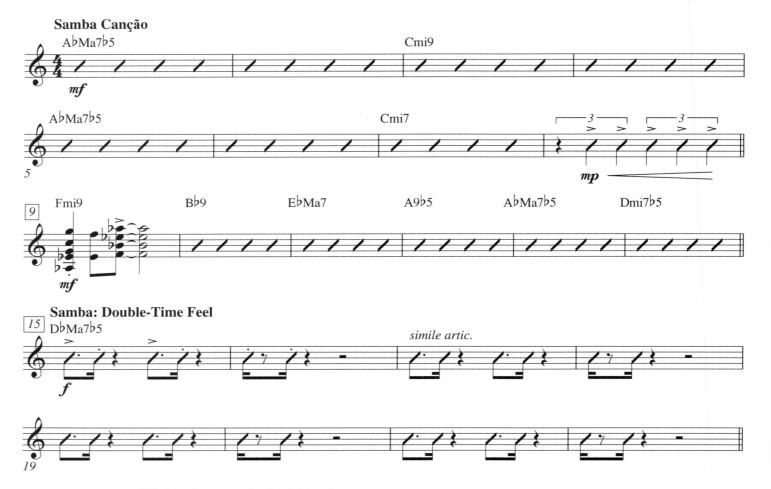

FIG. I.8. Samba with Slash Notation

Now that we've reviewed the rhythm section, the foundation of the band, let's jump into the horns!

CHAPTER 1

Agility and Speed: Saxophones

As a section, horns can supply a number of different options for your writing. As a group, they can do any of the following:

- play the melody (harmonized, unison, or octaves of unison)

- play unison or harmonized background lines

- perform horn *solis*: group horn solos

- play pads to add weight and color to your arrangement

- double other instrument parts for a bigger sound

We will discuss individual horn roles in the upcoming chapters.

Saxophones can play very quickly and can cover wide leaps easily. Notes are sounded by combining and varying the following:

- Speed and intensity of airflow the performer is sending through a rubber or metal mouthpiece to set a reed into motion to create an initial "buzzing" sound. Specific reed thickness and quality of the reed can greatly affect the instrument's sound.

- Pressing and releasing the instrument's keys and various key combinations to effectively shorten or lengthen the length of the airstream (lowering or raising the pitch)

- Embouchure (mouth shape around the mouthpiece). The embouchure helps to control tone, exact pitch, and a number of effects.

In terms of articulation, saxophones can play lightly as well as very forcefully. They can easily play short notes as well as long notes. The instrument is quite versatile in this regard. Perhaps a saxophone's only shortcoming is that it doesn't have a lot of power when compared to the brass. This shouldn't be considered a problem, though, as one goal for an arranger is to create music that makes great use of the instruments' strengths.

Saxophones can blend very well with other instruments in your band. For example, artists such as saxophone player Tom Scott have combined alto sax with distorted guitar. The buzz of the reed blends very well with some kinds of guitar distortion. On the other end of the saxophone family, the bari sax can be combined with an electric or acoustic bass to create another color in the bottom end. Ronnie Cuber and others have done this to great effect. In the middle of the saxophone section, one of my favorite tenor sax players, Ernie Watts, has combined that instrument with strings to come up with yet another interesting color. I encourage you to explore these possibilities and note their effect.

TRANSPOSITION

Many instrument players *read* pitches that are not the same as what the final *sounding* pitch is. Saxophones and trumpets fall into this category. These are known as "transposing instruments." Many horns and woodwinds in use today function this way. The main reasons for this are largely due to the construction of the instruments, their fingering relationships to other instruments in the same family, and to facilitate the reduction of ledger lines.

In this chapter, we focus on the saxophones.

There are four different saxophones in general use today. They are named like voices, from top to bottom: soprano, alto, tenor, and baritone. This chapter focuses on those most commonly found in most horn sections: the E♭ alto, B♭ tenor, and E♭ baritone or "bari." We'll look at fundamental issues regarding individual saxophones and their use as part of a horn section.

Other than being sure to write within an instrument's normal playing range, the most important thing to remember about wind instruments is the need to leave space for a player to breathe. Many people write music with computers today and forget that a line written in notation software may be impossible to play by a live musician!

E♭ ALTO SAXOPHONE

FIG. 1.1. Alto Saxophone

As mentioned previously, saxophones are transposing instruments. Alto sax notation is transposed a major sixth up from the concert pitch. For example, when the alto sax performer plays an A in their music, we hear the *concert* pitch C a major sixth *lower* than the written A. Figure 1.2 shows the range in both the concert notes (what the ear hears) and written or transposed notes for the player.

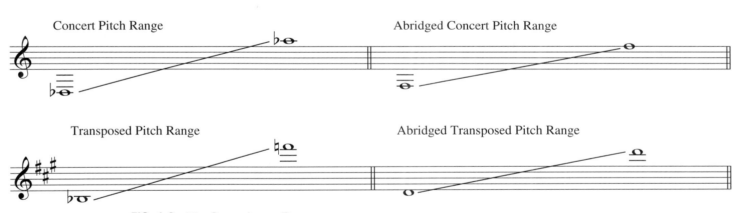

FIG. 1.2. Alto Saxophone Range

Additionally, note the "abridged range." This range is inside of the extreme highest and lowest notes of the instrument, where the player retains the most control over sound and dynamics (regardless of the performer's abilities). Unless you know the abilities of the specific player, it is safest to write within this range.

Figure 1.3 shows the different characteristics of the alto saxophone range.

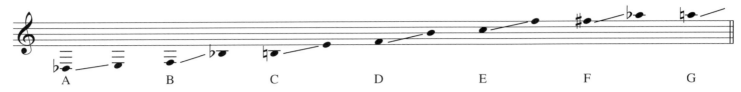

A   B   C   D   E   F   G

FIG. 1.3. Alto Saxophone Range Areas (Concert)

The "A" range is the very lowest, and the pitches here are difficult to produce consistently, especially when the dynamic level is below *f*. This area can, however, be used for special effects, particularly for soloists, as the instrument tends to sound like a "honk" here. Suggested dynamic range is *f* to *ff*.

Range "B" is a very strong and solid low area for alto. It has a nice round and clear sound. Blending capabilities with other instruments are very good, here. Projection of sound—the ability to be heard easily above other instruments—is also very good. Suggested dynamic range is *p* to *ff*.

The "C" range can be thought of as an upward added area to "B." The main difference is that the pitches don't have quite the same round sound as they do in the lower range. Projection is excellent. Additionally, notes are much easier to produce at soft dynamic markings in "C." Suggested dynamic range is *pp* to *ff*.

In range "D," the timbre of the instrument starts to really brighten up. The pitches, however, are still full. Projection is very good. Suggested dynamic range is *pp* to *ff*.

The brightest part of the alto sax's range is in "E." This area completes the octave started with range "D," and brings us to the top of the suggested abridged range for the instrument. Projection is excellent. Suggested dynamic range is *p* to *ff*.

The best areas for writing alto sax melodies are ranges C, D, and E.

Although many alto sax players can reach up to high A (concert) as the top end of their pitches, range "F" is the very top of the normal range for most players. For many, intonation and a general thinning of the sound can be problematic. Tone quality is quite bright. Unless you know that the alto player is a very experienced musician, it is best to avoid this area. Suggested dynamic range is *mp* to *f*.

The final area, range "G," is the beginning of what is known as the altissimo range and is not part of the normal range of the instrument. "G" is used quite often in improvisation and is a great high-energy timbre. Only the most skilled players attempt to sound notes in this range because the pitches are difficult to control. Musicians such as David Sanborn have made a very good living playing in this range. Needless to say, only write in this area after you have consulted with the player.

Figure 1.4 is an example of the alto sax playing through its range. Note how the instrument sounds thin and perhaps piercing when it is in its high range, but fuller and warmer when it is in its lower range. This transposed example is what the player is reading; the notes sound a major sixth lower. You can hear it on the accompanying audio.

FIG. 1.4. Transposed Alto Saxophone Example

Figure 1.5 is where the pitches in figure 1.4 will actually sound. The key signature is also a major sixth lower (B♭ rather than G).

FIG. 1.5. Concert Alto Saxophone Example

Noted alto saxophone players definitely worth looking into are Charlie Parker, Phil Woods, Cannonball Adderley, Paul Desmond, and contemporary players such as David Sanborn, Brandon Fields, and Bill Evans.

B♭ TENOR SAXOPHONE

FIG. 1.6. Tenor Saxophone

The B♭ tenor sax transposes up one full octave plus a major second higher than concert pitch. Thinking in reverse, the tenor player reads the note C but the pitch that is sounded is a B♭ an octave plus a whole step lower. Figure 1.7 illustrates the range as concert pitch, abridged pitch, transposed pitch, and transposed abridged pitch. Like the alto sax, some modern tenor saxes can go a half step higher in the range to E natural.

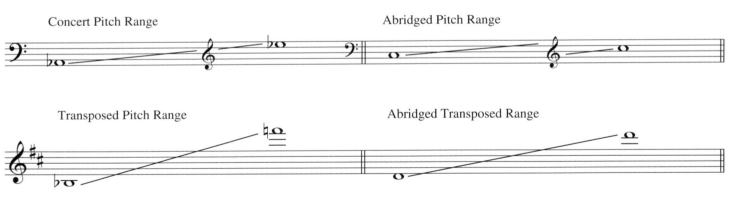

Concert Pitch Range   Abridged Pitch Range

Transposed Pitch Range   Abridged Transposed Range

FIG. 1.7. Tenor Saxophone Range

Figure 1.8 illustrates how the timbre changes, as the notes get higher. As discussed earlier, all instruments' tonal characteristics change throughout the range.

A   B   C   D   E   F   G

FIG. 1.8. Tenor Saxophone Range Areas (Concert)

Similar to the alto sax, in the tenor's "A" range, these pitches are difficult to produce consistently, especially when the dynamic level is below *f*. Having said that, the tenor sax, because it is built for the low end, is still more suited to this low area of the horn than the alto. This enables the instrument to have a slightly better sound in range "A." The area also can be used for special effects, particularly for soloists. Suggested dynamic range is *f* to *ff*.

Range "B" is the beginning of a very strong and solid low area for tenor. It has a nice round and clear sound. Blending capabilities, with other instruments, are very good in this area. Melodic and harmonic support is very good as is the projection of sound. Suggested dynamic range is *pp* to *ff*.

The "C" range can be thought of as an upward added area to "B." The main difference is that the pitches don't have quite the same round and full bottom sound as they do in the lower range. Projection is excellent. Additionally, notes are much easier to produce at soft dynamic markings in "C." Suggested dynamic range is *pp* to *ff*.

In range "D," the timbre of the instrument starts to really brighten up and can be a bit strident when compared to the lower areas. The pitches however are still round and full. Projection is very good. Suggested dynamic range is *pp* to *ff*.

As is the case with alto sax, the brightest part of the tenor's range is in "E." This area completes the octave started with range "D," and brings us to the top of the suggested abridged range for the instrument. Projection is excellent. Suggested dynamic range is *pp* to *ff*.

The best areas for writing tenor sax melodies are ranges C, D, and E.

Range "F" is the very top of the normal range of the instrument. Depending on the player, though, intonation and a general thinning of the sound can be problematic. Tone quality is quite bright. Unless you know that the tenor player is a very experienced musician, it is best to avoid this area. Suggested dynamic range is *p* to *ff*.

The final area, range "G," is the beginning of what is known as the altissimo range and is not part of the normal range of the instrument. Refer to my comments regarding range "G" in the alto sax discussion as they apply to this part of the tenor sax range as well.

Figure 1.9 is a transposed melody performed on tenor sax. Listen to the audio, and note that the instrument is overall lower in pitch than the alto, so it sounds "rounder" or "warmer."

FIG. 1.9. Transposed Tenor Saxophone Example

Figure 1.10 is where the notes actually sound. The key signature for the concert or sounding key can't be placed an octave plus a major second lower, but it can be placed a major second lower.

FIG. 1.10. Concert Tenor Saxophone Example

There are many great tenor sax players, but Stan Getz, John Coltrane, Lester Young, Michael Brecker, Dexter Gordon, Sonny Rollins, and Ernie Watts should be listened to for their tone and expressive qualities.

E♭ BARITONE SAXOPHONE

FIG. 1.11. Baritone Saxophone

The lowest pitched of the three saxophones is the E♭ baritone saxophone, or "bari" sax, which is transposed one full octave plus a major sixth higher than concert pitch. Traditionally, the bari sax could sound notes to D♭ concert, but it is common for today's instruments to sound low C concert. Figure 1.12 illustrates the range as concert pitch, abridged pitch, transposed pitch, and transposed abridged pitch.

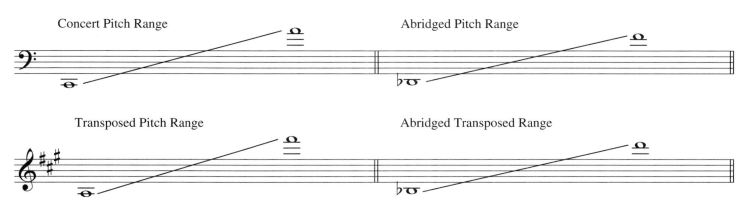

FIG. 1.12. Baritone Saxophone Range

Figure 1.13 illustrates how the timbre changes as the notes get higher. As opposed to the two other saxophones that we have discussed, the bari sax is built to play strong low notes. Therefore, most players can play in this area pretty easily. I like to think of the sound in this area as being big and round enough to build a house on! This is particularly true if one compares the sound of a trombone, for instance, playing these same notes. Volume is difficult to control below an *mf* marking unless the player is very experienced.

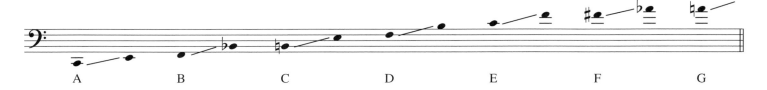

FIG. 1.13. Baritone Saxophone Range Areas (Concert)

The bari sax often anchors the low end of a voicing, and when coupled with electric or acoustic bass, works well for ostinatos or other repeated patterns. Keep in mind that in the "A" area, a great deal of air is necessary to produce the pitches. Projection is very good here. Suggested dynamic range is *mf* to *ff*.

Range "B" is an extension upward of range "A" but begins to lose some of the roundness and size of pitch that was present in the previous area. Blending capabilities and projection are both very good. Suggested dynamic range is *p* to *ff*.

The "C" range can be thought of as an upward added area to "B." The main difference is that the pitches don't have quite the same round sound as they do in the lower range. Projection is excellent. Additionally, notes are much easier to produce at soft dynamic markings in "C." Suggested dynamic range is *pp* to *ff*.

Range "D" is where the instrument really loses its role as the foundation of a voicing. The notes still sound rich and full when used properly in a voicing. Projection and blending capabilities are very good. Suggested dynamic range is *pp* to *ff*.

The next area of the bari sax's range is "E." This area completes the octave started with range "D," and brings us to the top of the suggested abridged range for the instrument. The tone starts to thin out in this area but is still clear. Projection is excellent. Suggested dynamic range is *pp* to *ff*.

Range "F" is the very top of the normal range of the instrument. Depending on the player though, intonation and a general thinning of the sound can be problematic. Tone quality is quite bright. Unless you know that the bari player is a very experienced musician, it is best to avoid this area. Suggested dynamic range is *p* to *ff*.

As was the case with alto and tenor, the final area, range "G," is the beginning of what is known as the altissimo range and is not part of the normal range of the instrument. Please refer to my comments in the alto sax section regarding this area.

Again, in figure 1.14, we have the original melody, this time played on bari sax. Listen to the audio, and notice how the overall sound is "thicker" and bigger than either the alto or tenor sax. This instrument is built for the low notes, as it sounds pretty big, especially below the treble clef.

FIG. 1.14. Transposed Baritone Saxophone Example

Figure 1.15 illustrates what the sounding pitches are. Like the alto sax, the bari's key transposes down a major sixth.

FIG. 1.15. Concert Baritone Saxophone Example

Figure 1.16 illustrates a comparison between the three saxophone ranges both in concert and transposed pitches. Note that the transposed ranges (what the player reads) are nearly identical. This is one of the reasons for having a transposed range. A saxophonist can pick up any of these instruments and have the same reading range.

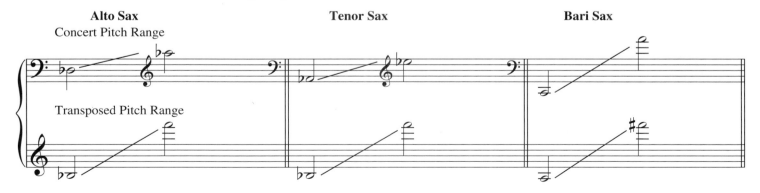

FIG. 1.16. Comparison of Saxophone Ranges and Transpositions

SAXOPHONE SECTION

Figure 1.17 is an excerpt from my composition "Toasted Hop." The score is in concert pitch so that you can see the actual notes the players are sounding. The alto has the "lead" or top voice. At the beginning, the tenor sax is playing unison, an octave below the alto sax, or at other times playing a "harmony part." As is often the case in horn writing, the bari sax plays an octave below the alto. This works well, as it strengthens the alto melody—the lead part. I've included a basic keyboard part so that you can see the harmony that was being played. Finally, as a technical scoring note, observe that the saxophones are braced together as they are in the same choir of instruments: the woodwind family.

Toasted Hop

FIG. 1.17. "Toasted Hop" Excerpt

Noted bari sax players include Gerry Mulligan, Serge Chaloff, Ronnie Cuber, Nick Brignola, and Doc Kupka.

CHAPTER 2

Power of the Horn Section: Trumpet and Trombone

The power of the horn section is in its brass instruments. This chapter will discuss two of the most common brass instruments in use today: the B♭ trumpet and the tenor trombone. You will occasionally see a bass trombone, tuba, French horn, flugelhorn, and others, but the B♭ trumpet and the tenor trombone are by far the most common brass instruments in contemporary jazz ensembles.

B♭ TRUMPET

FIG. 2.1. B♭ Trumpet

Like the saxophones (see chapter 1), the trumpet is also a transposing instrument. In this case, the transposition interval is a major second up from concert pitch. When the trumpeter reads a C in their music, the pitch B♭ will be sounded a major second *lower*. Figure 2.2 shows the range in both concert key (what the ear hears) and the written/transposed key for the player.

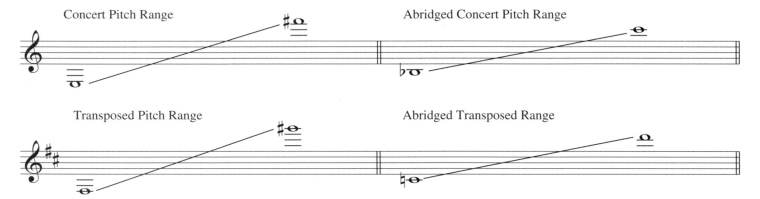

Concert Pitch Range   Abridged Concert Pitch Range

Transposed Pitch Range   Abridged Transposed Range

FIG. 2.2. B♭ Trumpet Range

The "abridged range" is also listed, where the player retains the most control over sound and dynamics. Unless you know the abilities of the specific player, it is best to write within this range.

Figure 2.3 illustrates how the trumpet's timbre changes throughout its range.

A   B   C   D   E   F   G

FIG. 2.3. B♭ Trumpet Range Areas (Concert)

In the very lowest range "A," the trumpet sound is not particularly clear and its projection is weak. This area might work well, however, as an effect for a soloist in a small group while the other musicians are playing softly. Suggested dynamic range is *p* to *mp*.

Range "B" is the area of most clarity and projection for the lower end of the trumpet. It has a nice round and clear sound. Blending capabilities with other instruments are also very good in this area. Suggested dynamic range is *pp* to *ff*.

The "C" range can be thought of as an upward added area to "B" or a lower extension of range "D." The trumpet really begins to brighten in tone in this area, but also can still play softly. Suggested dynamic range is *p* to *ff*.

Range "D" is generally considered the upper end of the trumpet for most small ensemble writing. This is particularly true when the writer is trying to maintain a good blend with a combination of horns such as the one we are exploring. As the trumpet goes higher, it begins to take over the overall sound of the group. Suggested dynamic range is *mf* to *ff*.

The remaining areas (E, F, G) are generally used in larger groups, such as big bands, which may have anywhere from three to five trumpets. These areas are also reserved for the best players. Endurance and control of pitch are problems that are difficult for the average player to control. The dynamic marking is "*ff*" or louder.

Notable trumpet players are Louis Armstrong, Dizzy Gillespie, Arturo Sandoval, Maynard Ferguson, Wynton Marsalis, Freddie Hubbard, and Wayne Bergeron.

Figure 2.4 is an example of the trumpet playing through its range. Listen to the audio, and note how the instrument sounds bright and piercing when it is in its high range, but fuller and warmer when it is in its lower range. The example is a transposed part; the notes sound a major second lower.

FIG. 2.4. Transposed B♭ Trumpet Example

Figure 2.5 is where the pitches from figure 2.4 actually sound. Note that the concert key signature is also a major second lower than that of the transposed part in figure 2.4.

FIG. 2.5. Concert B♭ Trumpet Example

TENOR TROMBONE

FIG. 2.6. Tenor Trombone

The tenor trombone is a nontransposing or "concert pitch" instrument, so the note the player reads is the same note that we hear. Figure 2.7 illustrates the range as concert pitch and abridged pitches. As was the case with other horns, the abridged or "inside" range is good to adhere to when you don't know the abilities of your players. Writing within the abridged pitch range also helps each instrument blend with each other, particularly in a small horn group.

Concert and Written Pitch Range   Abridged Pitch Range

FIG. 2.7. Tenor Trombone Range

More so than many instruments, the way a trombonist moves from pitch to pitch can be critically important to a writer. Trombonists use a combination of varying embouchure (lip buzz) and the trombone's slide to adjust the length of the instrument's tubing to produce different notes. In general, the lowest notes are created with the longest tubing and the highest notes are created with the shortest tubing. The slide can be moved to any of seven positions—as well as points between the positions to create longer or shorter tube lengths. Slide position 7 is the fully extended tube length whereas position 1, closest to the player, is the shortest tube length. Figure 2.8 illustrates the trombone's notes and its corresponding slide positions (though alternate positions are possible).

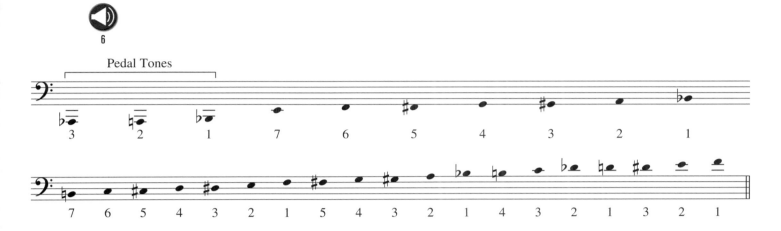

FIG. 2.8. Tenor Trombone Positions and Pedal Tones

Referring to example 2.8, the pedal tones A♭, A, and B♭ are well below the bass clef. The B♭ is secure and useable for most professional players. The A♭ and A are possible but can be weak, depending on the player. These pitches sound fuller and most secure on the bass trombone (a less common instrument), which has a larger bore and therefore fuller sound in this low area.

Starting with the pitch E below the bass clef, note how all seven positions are needed to sound the first octave of the chromatic scale. As the pitches get higher, fewer positions are needed. The way this affects the writer is this: If you write a C (6th position) and then a B♭ (1st position), and want the notes performed quickly one after the other, the player must move the slide from 6th position to 1st position very fast. Depending on tempo, it may actually be impossible to perform the passage. Being that much music is written with the aid of notation software today (which can play back anything you write), it is important to keep the slide position issue in mind when writing for this instrument, particularly in the first octave of the range. However, a trombonist may have an alternate slide position or trigger mechanism for a particular note, so when in doubt, always consult a player.

Figure 2.9 illustrates how the timbre, or sound, of the instrument changes as the notes get higher. All instruments' tonal characteristics change as pitches get higher.

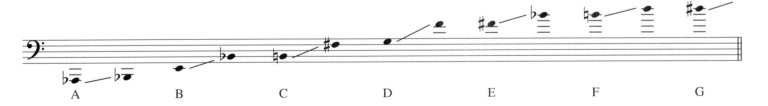

FIG. 2.9. Trombone Range

Although not exclusively, in the very lowest range "A," the pedal tones on the tenor trombone are often used for special effects. Experienced trombonists can create some very interesting sounds in this range. The five pitches from B natural up to E♭ separating range areas 1 and 2 are not possible without the aid of the mechanical trigger previously mentioned. Suggested dynamic range is *p* to *f*.

Range "B" is the area of most clarity and projection for the lower end of the trombone. It has a nice round and clear sound. Blending capabilities with other instruments are also very good in this area. Suggested dynamic range is *pp* to *ff*.

The next range "C" can be thought of as an upward added area to "B" or a lower extension of the next area, range "D." The trombone tone begins to brighten in this area, but also can still play softly. Suggested dynamic range is *p* to *ff*.

Range "D" is generally considered the upper end of the trombone for most small ensemble writing. This is particularly true when the writer is trying to maintain a good blend with a combination of horns such as the one we are exploring. As the trombone goes higher than this, it begins to take over the overall sound of the group. Suggested dynamic range is *mf* to *ff*.

The remaining areas (E, F, G) are generally used in larger groups, such as big bands, which may have anywhere from three to four trombones and sometimes even five. These areas are also reserved for the best players. Endurance and control of pitch are problems that are difficult for the average player to control. The dynamic marking is "*ff*" or louder.

A few trombonists I definitely would listen to for tone, improvisation, statement of melody, and technique would be contemporary players such as Bob Brookmeyer, Bill Watrous, Hal Crook, Carl Fontana, J.J. Johnson, Wayne Henderson, Grover Mitchell, Rob McConnell, and Arturo Velasco. Earlier trombonists that came out of the swing era would have to include innovators Glenn Miller, Tommy Dorsey, and Slide Hampton.

Figure 2.10 is the melody for a piece of mine titled, "Tangarablé," as played by a tenor trombone. The first six measures illustrate the first octave of the instrument. Notice how the sound is warm, round, and supportive. In measures 7 through 14, the sound changes and becomes focused, and it has a singing quality to it—a very nice area to play a melodic phrase, as it tends to cut through the rest of the band nicely.

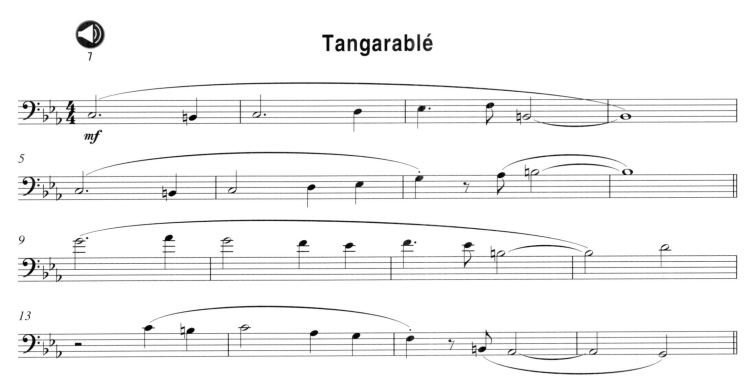

FIG. 2.10. Tenor Trombone Melody Example

MUTES

Trumpet, trombone, and other brass instruments sometimes use mutes to change their timbre. A mute is a device that fits into or over the bell. Mutes may be made of wood, metal, plastic, fiber, or rubber. There are many different kinds of mutes, and each one changes the sound differently, or allows the musician to control their sound in different ways.

The most common types of mutes are the cup mute and the Harmon (or wah-wah) mute. You will also find straight mutes, solotone mutes, whispa mutes, plungers (which are actual sink plungers), and others. Trumpet and trombone players usually have at least one or two mutes. Other brass instruments, such as French horn and tuba, have them more rarely.

In addition to changing the timbre, mutes also reduce the sound's volume. This is helpful for creating "offstage" effects, as well as for practicing in hotel rooms late at night. Loud dynamics with muted timbres can be achieved through amplification. Using mutes requires more breath, and as an arranger, you must be aware of this when writing phrase markings.

Mutes also affect instrument ranges, making them more difficult to control in terms of dynamics, intonation, and breath support. But using mutes, and carefully notating the specific effects that you require, can open up worlds of new timbral possibilities for your arrangements.

It takes a few seconds to insert or remove a mute, so ideally, give the player two measures to insert a mute or two bars to remove it, depending on the tempo of your music. This is particularly true with trombone players, who require both hands to play.

Using any mute is indicated in the score by the mute name, above the staff, as in "Cup Mute" or "Harmon Mute." To indicate that a mute should no longer be used, write "Open."

Figure 2.11 illustrates the various colors available when using mutes.

FIG. 2.11. Transposed Melody for Various Trumpet Mutes

Listed below are audio examples employing a variety of common mutes for trumpet. Listen to the phrase with no mutes employed first as a way to compare how the timbre changes.

Track	Mute
8	Original Phrase, No Mute ("Open")
9	Solotone Mute (1920s to 1930s jazz)
10	Soulo Mute, adjustable, positioned close to the bell of the trumpet
11	Soulo Mute, adjustable, positioned out from the bell of the trumpet
12	Straight Mute
13	Harmon Mute, adjustable stem in
14	Harmon Mute, adjustable stem completely out (Miles Davis sound)
15	Harmon Mute, with "wah-wah" effect
16	Cup Mute
17	Plunger Mute, half on with "wah-wah" effect

HORN SECTION

Now that we have examined all the horns individually, let's listen to them playing together. Figure 2.12 is an excerpt from the introduction to my piece "Toasted Hop," notated in concert pitch. The three saxophones start out the melody together in octaves. Trumpet 2 and the trombone enter in measure 3, essentially playing pitches already being performed by the saxophones. This gives the overall sound a little more "weight" and force. In measure 4, trumpet 1 is added but in a higher register than what has been played to this point. This added octave gives the horn section more weight, size, energy, and brilliance of overall sound. This is also known as an "orchestrated crescendo" because adding players and range can only make the music get louder when using these instruments—especially the brass.

When discussing the saxophones in the previous chapter, I mentioned that these instruments were braced together because they were in the same choir or family of instruments. In figure 2.12, however, note that I have braced the saxophones and trumpets together as one group of horns. The order is from potential highest note on top (Trumpet 1) to the potential lowest note of the group on the bottom (Bari Sax). This type of scoring makes it much easier to see all of the notes being used in a high to low order.

Toasted Hop

FIG. 2.12. "Toasted Hop" (Concert Score)

CHAPTER 3

Instrumental Roles: How to Implement the Horns

Horns can perform a variety of roles or jobs. Let's explore the different ways that they can be used in an arrangement, and then look at the specific possibilities of the individual instruments.

Before you start writing an arrangement, consider the instruments you will use and how you will use them. Whatever you decide at this point can be changed at any time, but at least you will have a good idea as to how you will proceed.

There are two major categories of roles that horns might play: melodic and accompaniment.

MELODIC ROLES

The melody tells the listener what the song is about. Melody is one role that any instrument in your band or ensemble can perform.

Written Melody

19

Listen to the audio clip from my song "And So It Goes," and consider how the flute is being used. We first hear a flute mixed with an alto sax to start the introduction. Then, once the rhythm section groove starts, the flute plays a melodic idea all by itself. Next, the alto sax plays the main melody up to the first solo section.

Now, listen to track 20 (figure 3.1), and consider what the trumpet is doing.

Toasted Hop

FIG. 3.1. "Toasted Hop" for Trumpet

Here, the trumpets are playing the melody. In both examples, we can tell which instruments are playing the melody because they are the most prominent and have a lyrical or sung quality to them.

Solos

There are two different types of solos that a performer can play: improvised and written. Both are opportunities for the performer to be featured and provide their creative point of view to the given musical material.

An *improvised* solo is spontaneous; the soloist creates the musical idea on the spot. Accordingly, every time that particular section of the arrangement is played in future performances, the solo will be different.

A *written* solo is scripted, note for note, by the arranger or composer. In traditional classical music, written solos are called "cadenzas," created by the composer as a way to feature the particular artist. Later, some performers wrote out their own cadenzas.

Shorter written out solos—as little as a couple of measures long—can also be created. These are generally meant as a means for a short phrase to be highlighted.

Listen to the following example, and note how the trumpet player performs this improvised or spontaneously created solo.

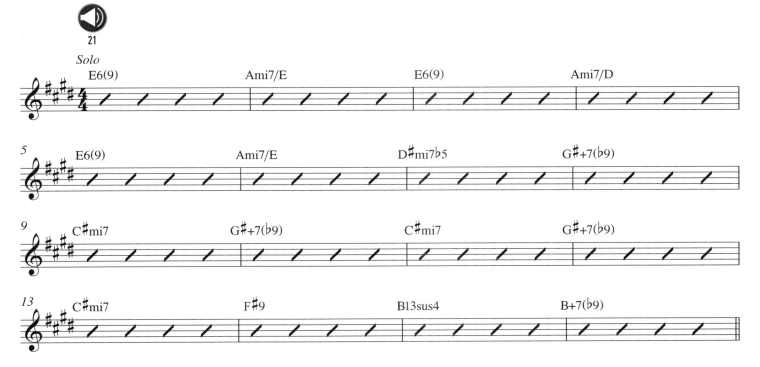

FIG. 3.2. Notation for Improvised Solo

Although melodic in nature, the pitches being played in track 21 constitute an improvised solo. The flugelhorn (a close relative to the trumpet) is playing notes from scales related to the chord symbols but in a way that is "of the moment," not written down in traditional notation. This area fits the role of an improvised solo. In rock, jazz, Afro/Cuban, Brazilian, and many other styles, the solos are often improvised by the specific performer.

Fills

Fills are great tools to add interest to your arrangement. This role tends to make a comment on the melody as a shortened improvisation or embellishment of the melody, without getting in the way. A fill may be useful when either the melody is resting or is holding a long tone, such as a whole or half note. It usually consists of a rhythm that is more active than the melody in that specific spot, so the fill is easily heard by the listener but is too short to be confused as the melody.

Listen to track 22 (figure 3.3), an excerpt from my song "Toasted Hop," that features fills in the horn section. Note where the fills occur.

Toasted Hop

Jerry Gates

FIG. 3.3. "Toasted Hop" with Horn Section Fills

ACCOMPANIMENT ROLES

So far, we've discovered the roles of melodies, solos, and fills that individual performers can perform within an arrangement. As an ensemble, several accompaniment roles are possible that can enhance an arrangement.

Pads

A *pad* is a vertical structure, or chord, that is often made up of long tones, such as half notes, whole notes, or tied whole notes. Pads "glue together" the overall band sound, offering harmonic support. Pads are normally heard in the background. Unlike a melody, fill, or solo, pads typically do not grab the listener's attention.

Listen to track 23 (figure 3.4), which features pads in the horn parts. As this is the introduction of the piece, the horn pad along with the rest of the ensemble are communicating the groove and overall feeling of the music to the listener. However, in this application, the pad *is* attracting attention because of the range of notes the trumpet is sounding. This pad also takes the edge off of the syncopation that is being created in the rhythm section. Finally, note the crescendo and decrescendo in the horns. In this simple technique, the horn pad gives a little more depth to the music. The listener may or may not notice, but I believe on a subconscious level, it makes a difference. When the section repeats, a bass solo is introduced that leads into the melody.

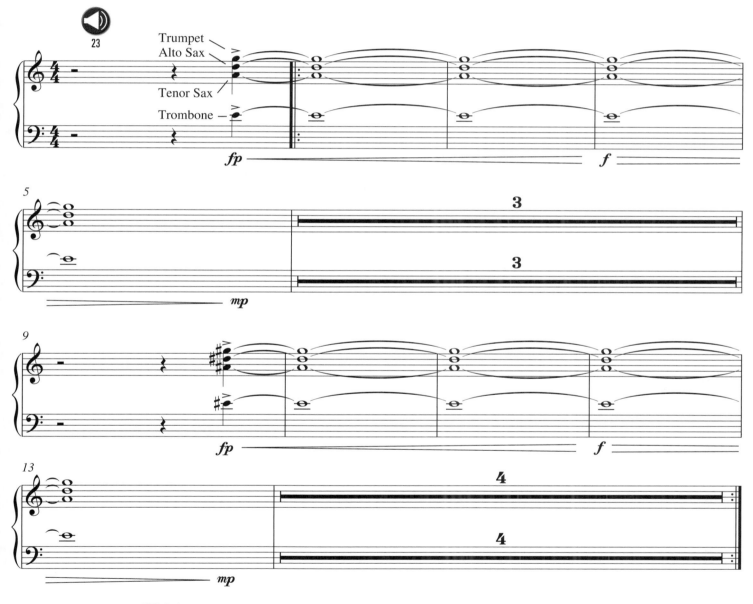

FIG 3.4. Horn Pads

Background Lines

In figure 3.5, the long-tone voicings are heard in the background and also provide an additional source of harmony for the arrangement. This brings us to a fifth role: the background line.

Background lines, also sometimes known as "guide tone lines," offer the arranger a couple of options. First, they are an added element that can help keep the listener interested in the music. It does this by being a secondary melody without being so prominent that it is confused with the melody. They also offer a way to lead the listener through the chord changes in a less-than-obvious way. Background lines are usually written in unison or octaves of unison, with a generous use of long tones. They primarily include 3's, 7's, and tension tones—the pitches that offer the greatest amount of interest.

Figure 3.5 is an example featuring a background line played by trombone and tenor sax. Note how the background line, illustrated below, is pretty directional. The target notes in this case are the thirds of each chord—often great choices, as they help to define the prevailing harmony. The rhythmic movement in the background line comes when the melody, played by the trumpet, is holding a note or resting. This allows neither the melody nor background line to conflict with each other.

FIG. 3.5. Horn Background Line

Comping

Finally, we have what is called "comping" (short for "accompaniment"). In this role, an instrument or group of instruments plays notes and rhythms that help define a groove or stylistic approach. In figure 3.6, the synthesizer is playing an improvised solo while the combination of trumpet and trombone, along with the rhythm section, supply a written out rhythmic pattern that helps to reinforce the chosen style. Additionally, the brass accompaniment supplies added contrast as the solo progresses.

Track 25 (figure 3.6) is from my song "Slammed," featuring horn comping.

FIG. 3.6. Comping Part to "Slammed"

Using these different instrument roles in your arrangements will greatly expand your creative options.

CHAPTER 4

Couplings in the Horn Section

Now that we've learned the basic capabilities and roles of our horn section, let's use them in an arrangement. Assigning a particular instrument to a pitch or pitches is known as "orchestrating." Using *couplings*—setting multiple instruments on the same melody—is one way to orchestrate. Let's look at the brass orchestration for the beginning of "Toasted Hop" in figure 4.1.

FIG. 4.1. "Toasted Hop" Brass Orchestration

OCTAVE/UNISON COUPLING

The strongest and most focused technique for stating any melodic idea is through the use of unison or octaves. When using more than one trumpet, putting all of them in unison works well. However, as the melodic line's range goes above the staff, it is best to put the trumpets in octaves ("octave coupling") because intonation in this range can become difficult. Additionally, for a bigger sound, playing in octaves creates more "orchestral size."

Figure 4.1 illustrates these simple, but powerful options. At the beginning of the example, the trumpets are in unison. The trombone's range is lower, so it is set in an octave coupling below trumpet 2, creating a stronger sound.

Figure 4.2 shows us another example of octave couplings, scored for trumpet, tenor sax, and trombone. The tenor sax's range is lower than the trumpet, so it's placed an octave below, joined in unison with the trombone. Another option would be to set the trombone an octave below the tenor, yielding a total of three octaves of the melody. However, in its upper range, the trombone is more focused and forceful, so I chose to set it higher.

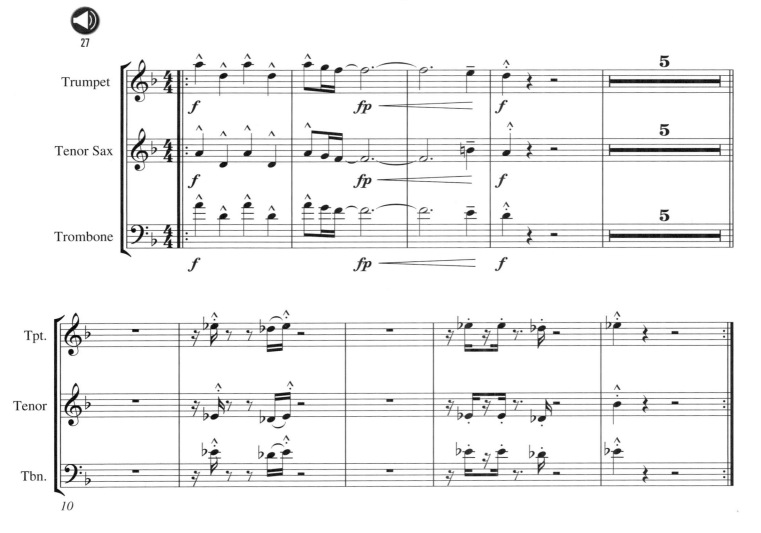

FIG. 4.2. Octave Coupling

DIATONIC COUPLING

Coupled lines can also be set using other intervals. Further into "Toasted Hop," the tenor sax alternates doubling in octaves and diatonic thirds below the melody. These thirds are always diatonic to the chord or key of the moment.

In measure 1, the alto and tenor saxophones are one octave apart, while the bari plays in unison with the tenor sax. In measure 3, note how the tenor sax jumps up to an interval of a third below the top note, creating 2-part harmony. This is an interesting variation to measure 1. Measure 5 uses the same coupling as measure 1, while measure 7 uses the same coupling as measure 3. Measure 8 shows the saxophones playing the coupling of a fifth between the alto and tenor sax. There are two octaves between the alto and bari sax, which strengthens the melody.

FIG. 4.3. Octaves and Diatonic Thirds

Any interval can be placed below a melody note, depending on the effect you would like to achieve. Octaves, diatonic thirds, sixths, fourths, and fifths are most common, however, as they create the least amount of dissonance.

Chromatic notes (notes that are not part of the key or chord of the moment) can be used as well, but they need to be handled carefully, as discussed in the next chapter.

CHAPTER 5

Horns in Triads

While unison and octaves give focus and power to a melody, harmonizing the line creates color and body. In chapter 4, we started adding color by coupling below the melody. Now, let's add more color and fullness as well, using a short melody in figure 5.1 as an example.

FIG. 5.1. Short Melody (To Be Harmonized)

SOLI VOICINGS

In figure 5.1, all the melody's notes are drawn from the chords indicated in the symbols above each note. In figure 5.2, we fill in the rest of the triad below each melody note. These are called "soli" voicings because all of the notes share the same rhythm. This is an arrangement for horns and bass.

FIG. 5.2. Soli Voicings

A number of items should be observed in figure 5.2:

- A bass line, playing each chord's root, is added to clarify the triads.

- The melody is always the top note of each voicing. This is because we hear the voicing's outside parts most easily.

- The chord symbols indicate four-part chords, but the horns here use three-part voicings (just the root, 3, and 5). Basic triadic voicings like these can work, though the lack of 7's and tensions may make the arrangement more characteristic of music from the 1930s and 1940s. We'll look at some ways to develop the sound.

CHORD STACKS

Here are the pitches that fully define our example's harmony. These structures are called *chord stacks*. A chord stack typically includes all of the notes, lined up vertically, that are included in the scale of the chord symbol. In this example, I am using only the chord tones from each chord symbol.

FIG. 5.3. Chord Stack

These chords have four notes, but in our arrangement, we only have three horns to play each structure. Figure 5.4 illustrates how to voice the chords so that a complete sound of each harmony will be heard. Note that in most cases, the root is not present in the voicing, but the bass is playing it.

FIG. 5.4. Chord Stacks: Leaving Out the Root

In figure 5.4, we moved beyond the basic triad sound. The melody can be harmonized with *any* triad contained within each chord stack, as long as the melody note is the root, 3, or 5 of the chosen triad. So, in measure 1 beat 2, there is a melody note A. If we look at the FMa7 chord stack in figure 5.5, we can see that there is also an A minor triad that uses the A as the root of that triad, as well as that F major triad we tried originally in figure 5.2, which uses the A as the 3 of the triad.

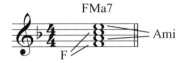

FIG. 5.5. FMaj7 Chord Stack

The F major triad originally chosen didn't allow the 7 of the chord (E) to be heard. However, choosing the A minor triad allows the E to be sounded. While there will be no root (F) in the horn voicing, in this case, the bass (or some other rhythm section instrument) will play the root, so the horns don't also need to include it.

The same technique was applied to the D (Gmi7), C (Ami7), and the D of the B♭Ma7 chord.

The last two notes of the melody (B♭ and F) must be handled differently because of their relationships to their respective chords.

FIG. 5.6. B♭ Melody

Looking at figure 5.4, you'll notice that there is a B♭ melody note in the second measure (the "and" of beat 3). The next chord tone below the B♭ is A, the 7 of the chord. The problem with this is that the interval between the B♭ melody note and the A below it is a minor second. When notes get that close to each other, it can be difficult to hear which is truly the top or melody note. To avoid this potential issue, we substituted the 6th degree of the B♭ major scale (G) for the 7 (A) as indicated in figure 5.6. Now, the distance between the two notes is farther and will not cause an unwanted dissonance.

The very last note of figure 5.4 (F) was handled in the same way. The note below the F (root of the FMaj7) should be an E, but this creates that minor second interval that we normally don't want, so the 6 of the scale is used instead of the 7.

Figure 5.7 illustrates another way to apply triads to measure 1. Here, the melody note is A, the note below it is the root F, and the third pitch is E, the 7 of the FMa7 chord. The distance between the second and third notes is a minor second, but this minor second is at the bottom of the voicing, so it will not cause any issues with the melody.

FIG. 5.7. Triads in Close Position

Up to this point, we have looked at arranging triads in what is called "close position." This simply means that the interval distance from the top note to the bottom note is one octave or less. For instance, in figure 5.7, we can see that the distances between the top notes and bottom notes of these triadic voicings are less than an octave. With the exception of the first voicing (FMa7), the top to bottom note interval is a sixth (major and minor sixth), as shown in figure 5.8.

FIG. 5.8. Close Positions Example 2

There are times when a triad's notes don't fit within the comfortable playing range of the instruments in our ensemble. In figure 5.9, there is a melody that I would like to harmonize.

FIG. 5.9. Melody Example

Harmonizing the melody in close position could look like figure 5.10.

FIG. 5.10. Melody Harmonization

This would work well if our instrumentation was trumpet, alto sax, and tenor sax because the notes would fit nicely into each instrument's range, as shown in figure 5.11.

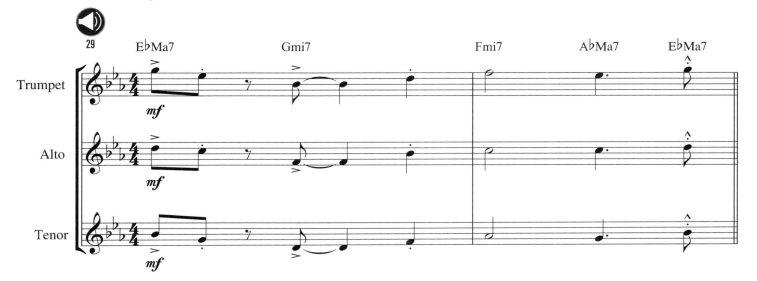

FIG. 5.11. Harmonization within Ranges of Instruments

But what if our ensemble was trumpet, tenor, and trombone? The lowest notes of our triads would be occasionally very high for the trombone (the tenor sax B♭s); its sound in that range might be too forceful compared to the trumpet and alto in their range. This could cause a blend problem within the ensemble.

The solution is to employ what is commonly called a "drop-2" voicing. Using this technique, the second note from the top of each close-position voicing is dropped down one full octave. The voicings would look like this:

FIG. 5.12. Drop-2 Voicing

Arranged for the trumpet, tenor sax, and trombone, it would look like figure 5.13:

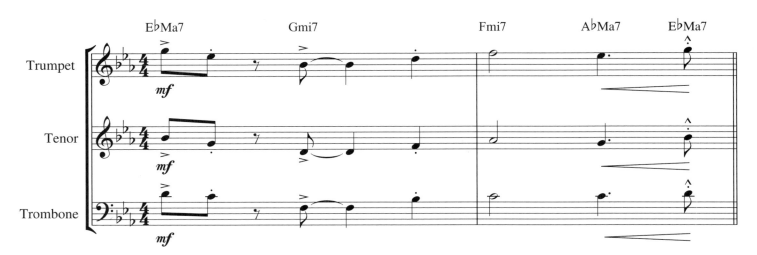

FIG. 5.13. Drop-2 Voicing Expanded

Figure 5.14 illustrates a close-position voicing option that puts both the tenor sax and trombone in very high ranges.

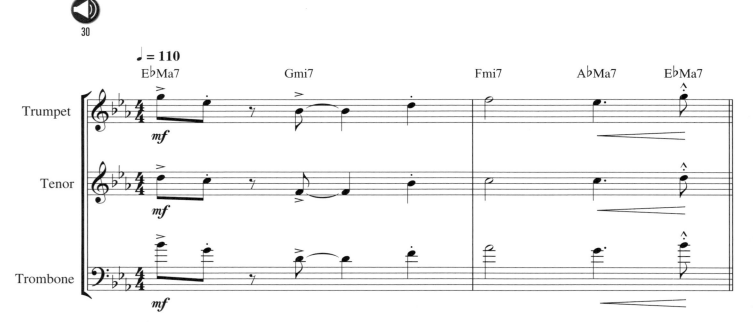

FIG. 5.14. Close-Position Version of Figure 5.13

A couple of things happened using the drop-2 technique. First, it put all three horns in a good range for them to sound their notes effectively. Second, the sound got bigger and "opened up" a bit, because all voicings now span more than an octave from the top pitch to the bottom. Applying this technique created voicings for these triads that are now anywhere from an octave plus a minor third to an octave plus a fourth. There are other voicings we can apply as well, but more on that later in this book.

CHAPTER 6

Four- and Five-Part Horn Voicings

At the beginning of the previous chapter, we voiced the horn section in triads. Let's add some additional horns and include more notes from the chord. Shown below in figure 6.1 is a piano reduction of what the notes were.

Figure 6.1 is the triadic harmonization in close position that we used in chapter 5. Looking at the example in a grand staff is often the easiest way to look at the notes involved. The three pitches could be applied to any three horns that can physically play the notes. Once we determine the notes we want to use we can then assign them to specific horns.

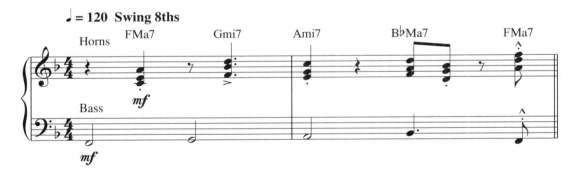

FIG 6.1. Close-Position Triads

The example was harmonized this way because we had three horns, so only three notes to assign to our horn section. Expanding each structure to accommodate four horns is fairly easy. Simply add the note that was missing from each voicing as a triad.

FIG. 6.2. Four-Way Close Position for Four Horns

If our horn section was comprised of trumpet, alto, tenor, and trombone, we could distribute the instruments on a concert pitch score like so:

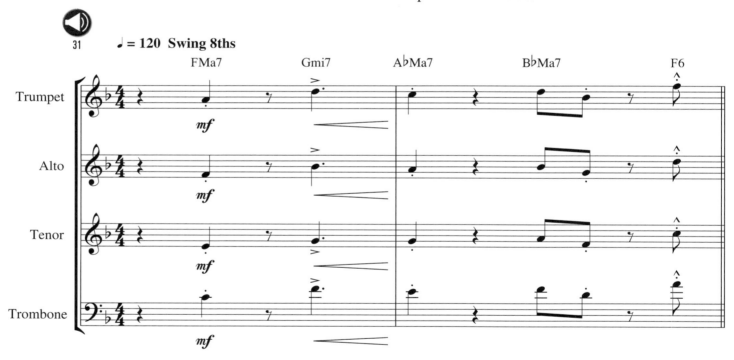

FIG. 6.3. Four-Part Harmonization for Trumpet, Alto, Tenor, and Trombone. Concert score.

To recap then, the decision on whether to use a close-position voicing versus a drop-2 voicing is range and sound. Drop-2 may facilitate a better range and blend for the chosen horns being used if the melodic range gets too high. A drop-2 voicing also opens up the sound a little bit enabling the horn combination to have a fuller sound. However, a close-position voicing has a tighter sound because of the proximity of each note to each other. Experimentation and experience with them both will help you determine when to use either. Additional techniques to write voicings exist, but first, let's look at one other topic, called "tension substitution," that can greatly enhance the sound.

TENSION SUBSTITUTION

Tension substitution is the practice of replacing a chord tone with a chord tension. Arrangers substitute tension for several different reasons. They may include:

- create a richer, contemporary sound from the horns

- better voice leading from chord to chord

- evoking a certain style and harmonic sound

Below is a basic list of chord qualities and the substitutions that are made. These are shown as a number with a slash and then another number. For example, "9/1" means that you can substitute the 9 of the prevailing scale for the root.

- Major chords: 9/1, ♯11/3, ♯11/5, 6/7

- Minor chords: 9/1, 11/3, 11/5, 6/7

- Dominant chords: ♭9/1, 9/1, ♯9/1, ♯11/5, ♭13/5, 13/5

Figure 6.4 illustrates the application of tension substitutions to figure 6.3.

FIG. 6.4. Tension Substitutions

Figure 6.5 is the application of four-part chords to the melody from chapter 5. No tension substitution is being used, with the exception of the second half of beat 1. Here, I've employed 6 (C) instead of 7 (D) to avoid the half-step interval on top of the voicing that would have occurred.

FIG. 6.5. Four-Part Chords

Here is the same example with tension substitutions applied to it.

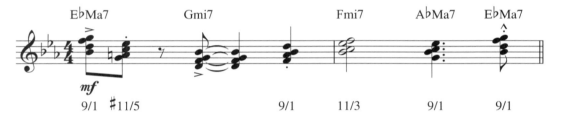

FIG. 6.6. Four-Part Chords with Tension Substitution

Tension substitutions should be applied with discretion. The coolest arrangement is not necessarily the one with the most tensions in it! Make sure it is the overall sound you want and that the notes below the melody make sense both vertically (harmonically) and horizontally (what each individual player is reading).

As we can see in figure 6.6, the notes are getting high in places. When we looked at triadic voicings, we solved this range issue by applying the drop-2 technique. This was a better range for the trombone, and it opened up the sound a bit. We can do the same thing with four horns as well.

FIG. 6.7. Drop-2 Voicings with Tension Substitution

Figure 6.8 illustrates the drop-2 technique with tension substitutions, arranged for four horns.

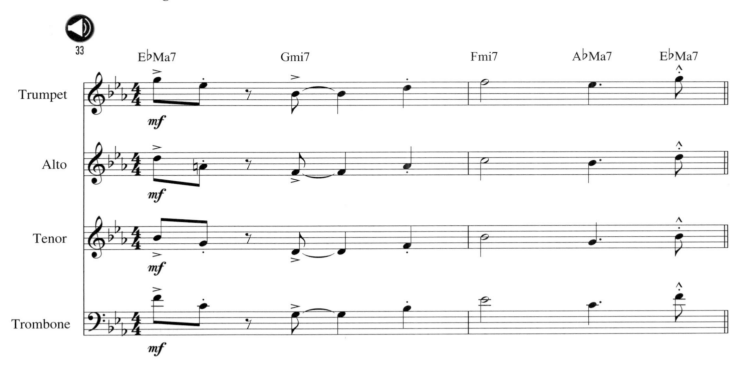

FIG. 6.8. Drop-2 Voicings with Tension Substitutions for Four Horns

FOUR-WAY CLOSE DOUBLE LEAD

Adding a fifth horn is not difficult, as long as you know what notes and tensions are available for each chord. We can start where we left off with four-part voicings. As an example, here's another simple melody with chord symbols.

FIG. 6.9. Melody with Chord Symbols

Figure 6.10 illustrates a harmonization of figure 6.9 using five notes in close position without tension substitutions. This is known as "4-way close double lead." The "lead" is the melody note doubled an octave lower.

FIG. 6.10. Four-Way Close Double Lead

Keeping the range of our horns in mind (trumpet, trombone, and alto, tenor, and bari saxes), we can also see that there are notes that may be quite high for some of the horn section to play. For example, in measure 2 beat 1, the pitch D is a half step away from the very highest note a tenor sax could play. In the last measure, the last voicing has a C♯ in it that may be very difficult for a trombonist to easily perform. As we did earlier in this chapter, we can apply a drop-2 technique to minimize this issue. The result of applying that technique looks like the example below.

FIG. 6.11. Drop-2 Double Lead

Scored out for five horns, it would look like this.

34

FIG. 6.12. Drop-2 Four-Way Doubled Lead for Five Horns (Concert Score)

With this expanded score, we can assign each instrument to specific notes. Comparing the individual instrument's ranges to the notes that are in figure 6.12, you'll note that the pitches fit the instruments ranges better, but there are still a couple of spots where, although the trombone and bari sax are not "too high," some improvements to their parts can still be made. An additional technique that can help is called "drop 2 & 4." Starting with a four-way close voicing, figure 6.13 illustrates the second and fourth voices are dropped an octave in the second measure. This not only opens up the sound even more than a drop-2 voicing, but potentially solves instrumental range limitations.

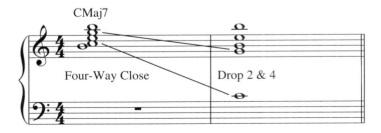

FIG. 6.13. Four-Way Close and Drop 2 & 4

Drop 2 & 4 technique is best employed when the melody notes are high.

Because of the wide interval of a drop 2 & 4 voicing, it isn't often applied to
melodic phrases that cover a wide area as well. However, we can apply it to parts
of a phrase to keep some instruments below the melody from getting too high,
as illustrated in figure 6.14.

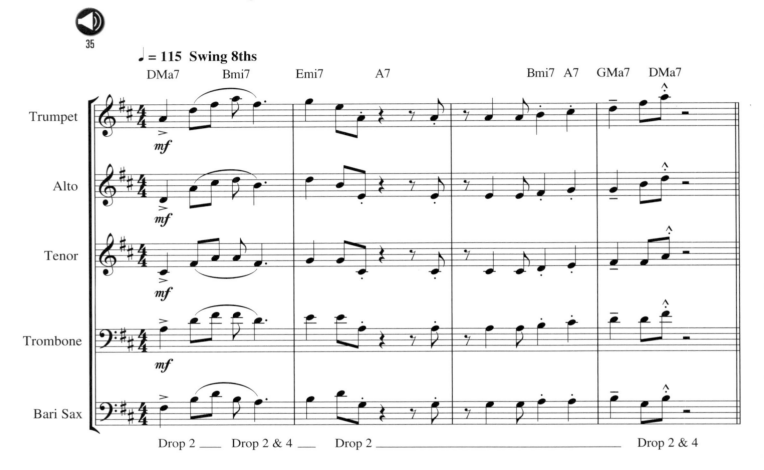

FIG. 6.14. Drop 2 & 4

Note that there was one tension substitution applied to the above example.
This is located in the very last note of the example in the bari sax part (B). The
note would normally have been a C♯, the 7 of the DMa7 chord. However, placing
the C♯ below the D in the alto sax would have caused a minor ninth interval to
occur. The minor ninth would not sound very good in this circumstance, so the
6 was substituted for the 7. There are additional spots we could apply tension
substitution to good effect as in figure 6.15.

FIG. 6.15. Drop 2 & 4 with Tension Substitution

Tensions add richness and color to the sound of this example. In particular, dominant chords should have at least a 9/1 and/or 13/5 substitution so that the overall sound is harmonically rich. Conversely, if you were working on a project that was to evoke early jazz (1920s to 1940s), you would not employ substitutions, as they weren't in common use yet.

CHAPTER 7

Approach Chords in the Horn Section

All of the examples used in the last three chapters have featured melodies that are chord tones of the chord symbol given. However, in addition to chord tones, many melodies use pitches that are not part of the chord symbol. These notes are called non-chord tones or "passing tones" because they typically pass between two strong chord tones. Passing tones are either *diatonic* or *chromatic* to the key or chord of the moment. First, we'll look at this topic as it might look on a piano and then expand to a horn section.

FIG. 7.1. Diatonic (DPT) and Chromatic (CPT) Passing Tones

In figure 7.1, the first non-chord tone, the E♭, is diatonic to the key signature of B♭ and the B♭ major scale, but is not a chord tone of the chord symbol B♭Maj7. In measure 2, the F is also part of the key signature of B♭, but is not a chord tone of E♭Ma7. Both the E♭ and F pitches are *diatonic passing tones*, as they are part of the scale for the key or chord symbols that are in force.

The same thing cannot be said of the A♭ at the end of measure 1. The A♭ is not part of the B♭ key signature nor is it part of the B♭Ma7 chord. This is called a *chromatic passing tone*. Chromatic passing tones are used throughout contemporary jazz, and, although not part of the scale, key, or chord symbol of a given moment, they can be used to great effect if they are resolved correctly, moving to a chord tone.

When harmonized, these passing tones in the different voices together form chords, and are thus called "approach chords," or "passing chords." How to harmonize a note that is not part of the chord symbol or key of the moment can be a big question mark, but it doesn't have to be. Consider the following:

- Chord tones are normally harmonized with notes drawn from the prevailing chord symbol. As we saw earlier, tension substitutions may be applied as well.

- Diatonic passing tones (non-chord tones) can be harmonized with any other chord that is part of the key of the moment, as long as the chosen chord includes the note you are trying to harmonize. This is called a diatonic approach chord.

- Chromatic passing tones can be harmonized with a chord that is the same chord quality as the target chord it is going to or approaching, either a half step above or below. This is called a "chromatic approach chord."

Figure 7.2 illustrates a simple five-part harmonization for the chord tones in the first example. It is a good practice to harmonize the chord tones first because then you know where the other pitches need to go.

FIG. 7.2. 5-Part Harmonization with Non-Chord Tones

Now, we need to harmonize the diatonic passing tones. As previously stated, approach chords are structures that can be used to harmonize diatonic or chromatic passing tones. Figure 7.3 presents one option for an approach chord in measure 1. The melody note E♭ is moving from below, by diatonic step, to the F. The next step is to choose diatonic notes below the E♭ that will move by diatonic step from below, like the melody, into their closest target pitch (the next closest chord tone). The approach chord's C moves up to the chord tone D, its A moves up to B♭, the G moves up to A, and the E♭ moves up to F. Keep in mind that all of the notes move in the same direction as the melody.

FIG. 7.3. 5-Part Harmonization with Non-Chord Tones Continued

This harmonization is very smooth, as all of the pitches in the approach chord are from the key of the moment and the B♭ major scale. For analysis purposes, the approach chord we created under the E♭ is an A–7♭5, which is also the VII chord in B♭ major. Because of this relationship, the A–7♭5 is called a *diatonic approach chord*.

Figure 7.4 illustrates the F in measure 2 harmonized. The same procedure as in measure 1 was followed. The F melody note is moving up to G, the chord tone and major third of the E♭Ma7 chord. The D below it moves up to the E♭ and the C moves upward to D. Finally, the A moves up to B♭ and the lowest note F moves up to G. The chord arrived at is a Dmi7. It works very smoothly because all notes are from the B♭ major scale. Again, we've employed a diatonic approach chord.

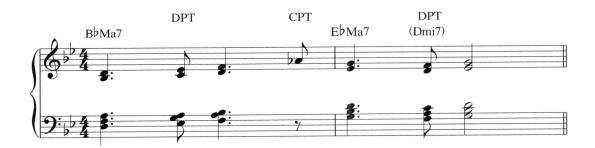

FIG. 7.4. 5-Part Harmonization with Non-Chord Tones Continued

CHROMATIC APPROACH NOTES

Let's look at the A♭ at the end of measure 1 in figure 7.4. As mentioned earlier, this note is neither a scale tone of the key of B♭ nor a part of the B♭Ma7 chord. For me, the easiest way to harmonize this note is to think of parallel motion between the A♭ and the target note G in the next measure. The target G note has already been harmonized as a chord tone of E♭Ma7. It is a simple matter, then, to make all of the notes below the A♭ move to their target pitches below the G from above, like the melody, by half step. Figure 7.5 demonstrates this procedure. It is often called a "chromatic approach."

FIG. 7.5. Chromatic Approach Example

Here's how the voices move in figure 7.5, under that A♭ in the melody.

- F♭ moves down to E♭.

- E♭ moves down to D.

- C♭ (B) moves down to B♭.

- A♭ moves to G.

In figure 7.6, technically, the chord we arrived at for the A♭ pitch is F♭Ma7 because of all the flatted notes (downward movement). We could also think of it as EMa7, the enharmonic equivalent of F♭Ma7, so there are fewer flats to think about. However, the added naturals and sharps can be confusing too, especially in a flat key, so use this option carefully.

FIG. 7.6. Chromatic Approach Continued

Figures 7.7 and 7.8 illustrate two different ways that we could apply the exercises we've just completed to a five-horn ensemble. Note the difference in sound when the alto sax is on top and the trombone is on the bottom. How does the timbre or color change?

FIG. 7.7. Trumpet on Top of the Voicing

FIG. 7.8. Alto Sax on Top of the Voicing

Contour Analysis of an Arrangement

39

Throughout *Arranging for Horns*, I have used examples from my song, "Toasted Hop." Let's now take a look at the structure of it, some of the questions I faced, and the decisions I made along the way.

I'm a big fan of thinking about what it is I want to achieve with a particular arrangement *before* I start writing pitches. Here are a few important things to think about as you conceptualize the arrangement:

- tempo

- key

- instrumentation

- audience (live performance, CD, radio, television, film, Internet, etc.)

- contour (how the arrangement might unfold)

- soloist(s) and what instrument that might be

- deadline for the arrangement to be completed

In the case of "Toasted Hop," I knew from the beginning that I wanted a big horn sound and that a swing sixteenth/hip-hop groove would be fun and energetic. The tempo would be between 90 and 110 beats per minute. I also knew that the piece was to be an instrumental song that will have a horn section that consists of three brass instruments (two trumpets and one trombone) plus three saxophones (alto, tenor, and bari). To this point in the book, we have only discussed five horns. However, you will find that the added horn, which is a second trumpet, is generally doubling a note that is already being played by one of the other horns. The added trumpet also gives me the ability to form a full triad with the brass. Beyond the horns, I would include a rhythm section. All of the band members for this arrangement were very good players, so writing sections for improvised soloing would be included. Finally, the deadline was also in place as the arrangement would be for a live performance in a concert hall. The first rehearsal was a week before the performance, so the first rehearsal became the deadline.

The next thing for me was to think about the contour or shape of the arrangement. If an arrangement does not have a clear shape, the audience members very likely will not respond positively.

In figure 8.1, we chart a composition's shape, with 0 being silence and 10 being the loudest possible volume and highest level of intensity. If the intensity of our arrangement is roughly a level 3 or 4, the listener might be bored, because nothing changes during its three-minute length. The music does not get louder or softer during this time.

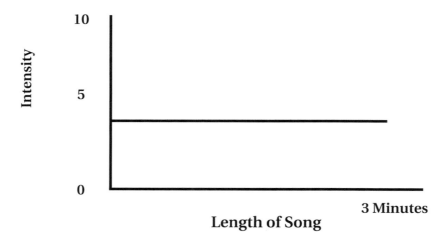

FIG. 8.1. Contour Analysis 1

Another contour shape is shown in figure 8.2. With this approach, the music starts out very loud and intense, but gets less so as the arrangement proceeds. This approach would not be optimum either, as we've given the loudest, most intense part of the arrangement to the listener at the very beginning. This would leave the listener with an expectation of something (more volume or intensity later in the arrangement) that they would never get from this contour.

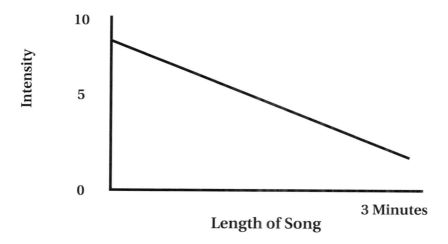

FIG. 8.2. Contour Analysis 2

In the setting of figure 8.3, the music starts softly and builds as the arrangement progresses. The big payoff is at the end. This is a common contour for pop music today. It works well because it adds intensity as the arrangement progresses.

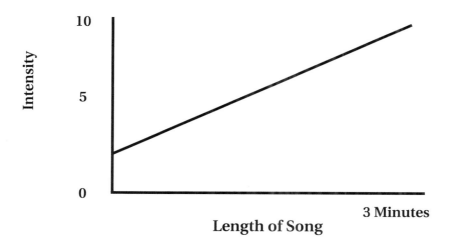

FIG. 8.3. Contour Analysis 3

A variation of this option is in figure 8.4. Here, the introduction starts big, gets soft for the first verse, and progressively gets bigger. Again, the big payoff, the most intense part of the arrangement, is at the end.

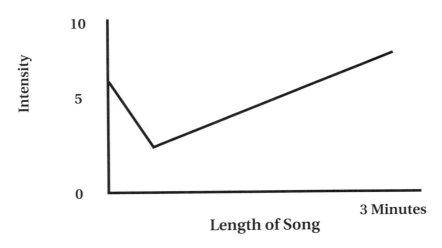

FIG. 8.4. Contour Analysis 4

The contour examples in figures 8.3 and 8.4 are not the only possible effective techniques to use in shaping your arrangement. However, keep the following in mind: The big, climactic part of your arrangement should not occur sooner than 75 percent of the way through it. More often than not, the biggest part of the song happens somewhere near or at the end.

Looking at "Toasted Hop," the arrangement starts out with drums and percussion informing us of the groove. Immediately, the listener knows what the style and basic feeling of the music will be. This is one of the characteristics of an introduction—to give the audience a sense of the music's style to be performed. After four measures, keyboard 2, guitar, and bass enter. This entrance gives the listener something additional to listen to, so it will hold their attention for a few moments more.

Toasted Hop

Jerry Gates

FIG. 8.5. "Toasted Hop" Intro, for Contour Analysis

Figure 8.6 is the addition of the horns to the final four measures of the introduction to "Toasted Hop." While the rhythm section is continuing their groove, the saxophones now enter in octave-unison. Note that I'm saving the brass until the very last two measures because the brass instruments represent power, especially in the very last measure where trumpet 1 is in its high register.

FIG. 8.6. "Toasted Hop" Additional Horns

As you'll notice in the recording, the melody starts at measure 13 (brassy synthesizer sound), but the horns continue and follow a decrescendo. This is called an "overlap" in the horns. An overlap is created when a melodic idea starts before the double bar line (end of a section) and ends after the double bar line, which is the beginning of a new section. An overlap helps the ear transition smoothly from one section to the next.

The process of adding instruments throughout the introduction creates its own contour. The contour peaks momentarily at the end of measure 12 and goes back down via the decrescendo and the omission of the horns at the end of measure 14. This allows me to start the building process all over again, but from a different starting level.

Measure 13 of figure 8.7 is where the melody starts, being played by Keyboard 1. The sound coming from the keyboard synthesizer is an old analog brass sound. At this point, the horns are not playing, so the level of the contour is lower. However, note that there are horn parts that say "2nd Time Only." This section of the arrangement will get repeated as the music progresses. On the repeat is where the horns will play these notes.

FIG. 8.7. "Toasted Hop" Measures 13–20

The next section of the song, illustrated in figure 8.8, is the "B" section of the song. The groove changes here; the Guitar plays harmony notes to Keyboard 1's melody. Horns will not play in this section until the second time through. The segno sign indicates that this section will be played a third time, after the solos.

FIG. 8.8. "Toasted Hop" B Section

FIG. 8.9. "Toasted Hop" Solo Section Measures 31–40

Although a rock guitar solo is played in measures 31–40, this section really acts as an interlude or bridge into the next section, which is the main solo for the arrangement. Both trumpets are playing the melody to give a little more weight of sound to the melody. If you compare the pitches in the horn voicings to the chord symbols, you'll also note that the voicings are incomplete. The third of each chord is often missing. Not to worry, this was intentionally done to get a certain sound quality created by omitting these notes. Again, the last section created its own peak.

After the guitar solo ends, the music again drops down to basic rhythm section to begin the piano solo. Looking at the full score, this is measures 41–48. I will add remaining players whenever I want the size of the sound to grow.

During the next twelve measures (figure 8.10), the saxophones enter, starting in octaves and answering the first phrase as two-part harmony that was discussed in chapter 5. As we found, the phrases get progressively longer in every four-measure section.

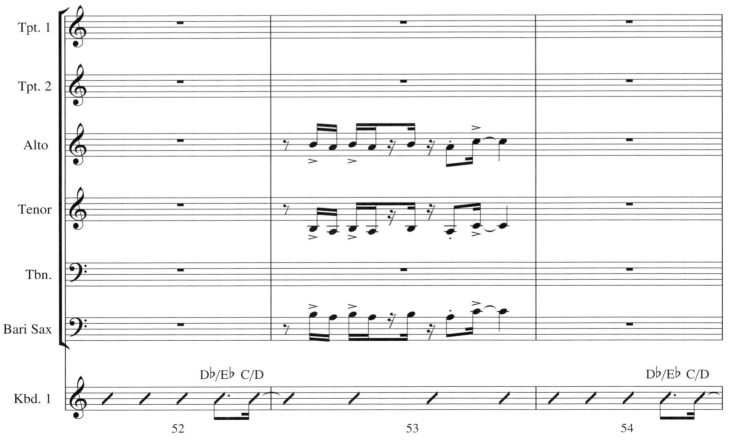

FIG. 8.10. "Toasted Hop" Measures 49–60

By increasing the length of each phrase, the intensity level behind the soloist continues to grow. The following techniques can be used to add intensity:

- add rhythms

- add instruments

- add melodic ideas (unison counter melodies, fills, or background lines)

- add octaves to a specific line

- add higher level dynamics

Next, the overall solo section continues to grow by adding the brass using a different rhythm and eventually adding an octave above the original idea at measure 68. Here, Trumpet 1 moves to an octave above Trumpet 2 to add size, brilliance, and intensity to the overall solo section. In the audio example, you can also hear that the soloist has moved from an electric piano sound to a brassy analog synthesizer sound to continue the upward intensity of the solo section.

FIG. 8.11. "Toasted Hop" Measures 61–69

This section is the arrangement's peak, and so the final section of the solo involves moving to the chords of the "B" part of the song to help bring the solo to a close (as illustrated in figure 8.12).

FIG. 8.12. "Toasted Hop" Measures 69–77

Finally, the horn section states the melody. Although there are times when a soloist may immediately restate the melody after the improvisation is complete, I prefer to let the soloist take a break for a moment. This lets the player rest after the solo, but also gives the listener's ears a break from that particular sound and allows the melody to be presented in yet a different way.

FIG. 8.13. "Toasted Hop" Measures 77–85

From this point, the arrangement takes the D.S. al Fine direction back to the segno sign (measure 21). Keyboard 1 again plays the melody. The horns play the background figures and fills just as they did in the second verse and chorus earlier in the arrangement. The arrangement is complete after a second rock guitar solo, and all instruments arrive very loudly at the "Fine" in measure 40. A complete version of the score and audio for this song is available online with the other media files. (See the first page of this book for the access code and URL.)

Throughout the arrangement, the overall contour progressively moves higher. The contour starts low and gets higher within sections as well. This is particularly true within the keyboard solo section, but also when comparing verse 1 to verse 2. Thinking about the arrangement's contour is very much part of the craft of the arranger. A solid contour can be the difference between an average arrangement and a very good one. An arrangement that leaves the listener satisfied is the goal ultimately.

WHAT'S NEXT?

One thing I've learned over the years is that the answers to our musical questions don't come in just one book or course or person. We learn about our craft over the course of a career through many resources. Hopefully, the information contained in this book has helped answer some of your musical questions and will aid you in your career path.

This isn't the end of your studies, of course. The next thing is to keep learning as much as you can about the language of music. Ask a lot of questions of other musicians that you think may be able to help. Listen to a lot of music, and try to listen critically to what you are hearing. Acquire scores to analyze whenever possible. This will go a long way toward helping you achieve your career goals and perhaps open many doors. Good luck to you, and feel free to contact me!

82

GLOSSARY

approach chord	vertical grouping of notes that harmonize an approach note or passing tone
approach note	a note that is a non-chord tone. It could be chromatic or diatonic to the key or chord of the moment.
chromatic pitch	a pitch or note that is not part of a key or scale at a given point in a piece of music
concert pitch	the pitch we hear when sounded
contour	a graphic look at how an arrangement progresses, usually showing the rise and fall of volume and/or intensity
diatonic pitch	a pitch or note that is part of a key or scale at a given point in a piece of music
dynamic range	the lowest to highest volume that an instrument can normally perform at
dynamics	symbols used to indicate a relative volume level that a player should perform their music
horns	in a band, collectively a group of brass and/or woodwind instruments; this is a different usage of the term than in an orchestra where a "horn" is a specific brass instrument
orchestral size	number of octaves being sounded at a given point in the music
orchestral weight	the number of instruments playing at any particular time
soli voicing	voicing whereby all of the notes involved are of the same rhythm
solo	in the context of a horn band, this means an improvised performance by a specific instrument or instruments
transposed/written pitch	pitch the player reads to sound a particular note
voicing	a specific vertical grouping of pitches that, when played together, form an intended harmonic sound

ABOUT THE AUTHOR

Photo by Alexandria Pierre Etienne, Ali Photography

JERRY GATES

Composer, educator, orchestrator, arranger, and producer Jerry Gates has been a music industry professional for over thirty years. At Berklee College of Music, he teaches in the contemporary writing and production department and has taught most of the core classes in that major. At the rank of professor, he teaches *Contemporary Arranging Techniques, Directed Studies in Arranging, Contemporary Twelve-Tone Composition, Orchestration*, and *Writing and Production in the Recording Studio.* He is author of the online courses *Arranging: Rhythm Section and Horns, Arranging: Advanced Horns,* and *Writing for Woodwinds and Strings* for Berklee Online, the continuing education division of the college. He is author of the book *All Twelve: Dodecaphonic Sources for Contemporary Composition* (2010). Additionally, Jerry teaches writing techniques such as contemporary composition, orchestration, and arranging privately through his website, www.jerrygatesmusic.com.

Jerry's most recently completed projects include producing and orchestrating string sessions for noted Egyptian producer/*Arab Idol* judge Hassan El Shafei and creating symphonic jazz arrangements for the Polish/German jazz group, Poetic Jazz. He has also composed, arranged, and produced music for Nestlé's' "Wonk Your Room" and Wonka.com's "Loss for Lyrics" online promotions.

Jerry's television and radio credits included commercials for Bank of America, Log Cabin maple syrup, Scope mouthwash, Marlboro cigarettes, and music preparation for *The Dennis Miller Show*, jazz great Bill Holman, and film composers Jack Smalley and Richard Band.

Jerry holds a bachelor of music from Berklee College of Music, a master of music/composition degree from the Hartt School at the University of Hartford, and also graduated from both the Television/Film Scoring and Composing/Arranging programs at the former Grove School of Music in Los Angeles, CA.

Examples of Jerry's current work can be found at:

- www.jerrygatesmusic.com

- soundcloud.com/jerrygatescomp

- www.reverbnation.com/jerrygates

- www.myspace.com/compjgates

INDEX

Note: Page numbers in *italics* indicate illustrations.

More Fine Publications from BERKLEE PRESS

GUITAR

BEBOP GUITAR SOLOS
by Michael Kaplan
00121703 Book..$14.99

BERKLEE BLUES GUITAR SONGBOOK
by Michael Williams
50449593 Book/CD..............................$24.99

BLUES GUITAR TECHNIQUE
by Michael Williams
50449623 Book/CD..............................$24.99

BERKLEE GUITAR CHORD DICTIONARY
by Rick Peckham
50449546 Jazz.......................................$10.99
50449596 Rock......................................$12.99

BERKLEE JAZZ STANDARDS FOR SOLO GUITAR
by John Stein
50449653 Book/CD..............................$19.99

THE CHORD FACTORY
by Jon Damian
50449541 ....$24.95

CREATIVE CHORDAL HARMONY FOR GUITAR
by Mick Goodrick and Tim Miller
50449613 Book/CD..............................$19.99

FUNK/R&B GUITAR
by Thaddeus Hogarth
50449569 Book/CD..............................$19.95

GUITAR CHOP SHOP – BUILDING ROCK/METAL TECHNIQUE
by Joe Stump
50449601 Book/CD..............................$19.99

JAZZ IMPROVISATION FOR GUITAR
by Garrison Fewell
A Harmonic Approach
50449594 Book/CD $24.99
A Melodic Approach
50449503 Book/CD Pack $24.99

A MODERN METHOD FOR GUITAR
by William Leavitt
Volume 1: Beginner
50449400 Book......................................$14.95
50449404 Book/CD..............................$22.95
50448065 Book/DVD-ROM $34.99
Volume 2: Intermediate
50449410 Book......................................$14.95
Volume 3: Advanced
50449420 Book......................................$16.95
1, 2, 3 Complete
50449468 Book......................................$34.99
Jazz Songbook, Vol. 1
50449539 Book/CD $14.99
Rock Songbook
50449624 Book/CD $17.99

PLAYING THE CHANGES: GUITAR
by Mitch Seidman and Paul Del Nero
50449509 Book/CD $19.95

THE PRACTICAL JAZZ GUITARIST
by Mark White
50449618 Book/CD................................$19.99

THE PRIVATE GUITAR STUDIO HANDBOOK
by Michael McAdam
00121641 Book......................................$14.99

BASS

BASS LINES
by Joe Santerre
50449542 Fingerstyle Funk:
   Book/CD..............................$19.95
50449478 Rock: Book/CD $19.95

FUNK BASS FILLS
by Anthony Vitti
50449608 Book/CD $19.99

INSTANT BASS
by Danny Morris
50449502 Book/CD $14.95

READING CONTEMPORARY ELECTRIC BASS
by Rich Appleman
50449770 Book......................................$19.95

DRUMS

BEGINNING DJEMBE
by Michael Markus & Joe Galeota
50449639 DVD......................................$14.99

DOUBLE BASS DRUM INTEGRATION
by Henrique De Almeida
00120208 Book......................................$19.99

DRUM SET WARM-UPS
by Rod Morgenstein
50449465 Book......................................$12.99

DRUM STUDIES
by Dave Vose
50449617 Book......................................$12.99

EIGHT ESSENTIALS OF DRUMMING
by Ron Savage
50448048 Book/CD $19.99

PHRASING: ADVANCED RUDIMENTS FOR CREATIVE DRUMMING
by Russ Gold
00120209 Book......................................$19.99

WORLD JAZZ DRUMMING
by Mark Walker
50449568 Book/CD $22.99

KEYBOARD

BERKLEE JAZZ KEYBOARD HARMONY
by Suzanna Sifter
50449606 Book/CD $24.99

BERKLEE JAZZ PIANO
by Ray Santisi
50448047 Book/CD $19.99

CHORD-SCALE IMPROVISATION FOR KEYBOARD
by Ross Ramsay
50449597 Book/CD Pack....................$19.99

CONTEMPORARY PIANO TECHNIQUE
by Stephany Tiernan
50449545 Book/DVD $29.99

HAMMOND ORGAN COMPLETE
by Dave Limina
50449479 Book/CD $24.95

JAZZ PIANO COMPING
by Suzanne Davis
50449614 Book/CD $19.99

LATIN JAZZ PIANO IMPROVISATION
by Rebecca Cline
50449649 Book/CD $24.99

SOLO JAZZ PIANO – 2ND ED.
by Neil Olmstead
50449641 Book/CD..............................$39.99

VOICE

THE CONTEMPORARY SINGER – 2ND ED.
by Anne Peckham
50449595 Book/CD $24.99

VOCAL TECHNIQUE
featuring Anne Peckham
50448038 DVD......................................$19.95

VOCAL WORKOUTS FOR THE CONTEMPORARY SINGER
by Anne Peckham
50448044 Book/CD $24.95

TIPS FOR SINGERS
by Carolyn Wilkins
50449557 Book/CD $19.95

YOUR SINGING VOICE
by Jeannie Gagné
50449619 Book/CD $29.99

WOODWINDS

FAMOUS SAXOPHONE SOLOS
arr. Jeff Harrington
50449605 Book......................................$14.99

IMPROVISATION
by Andy McGhee
50449810 Flute.....................................$14.99
50449860 Saxophone $14.99

THE SAXOPHONE HANDBOOK
by Douglas D. Skinner
50449658 Book......................................$14.99

SAXOPHONE SOUND EFFECTS
by Ueli Dörig
50449628 Book/CD $15.99

ROOTS MUSIC

BEYOND BLUEGRASS

Beyond Bluegrass Banjo
by Dave Hollander and Matt Glaser
50449610 Book/CD $19.99

Beyond Bluegrass Mandolin
by John McGann and Matt Glaser
50449609 Book/CD $19.99

Bluegrass Fiddle and Beyond
by Matt Glaser
50449602 Book/CD $19.99

THE IRISH CELLO BOOK
by Liz Davis Maxfield
50449652 Book/CD $24.99

BERKLEE PRACTICE METHOD

GET YOUR BAND TOGETHER
With additional volumes for other instruments, plus a teacher's guide.

Bass
by Rich Appleman, John Repucci and the Berklee Faculty
50449427 Book/CD $14.95

Cello
by Matt Glaser and Mimi Rabson
00101384 Book/CD $14.99

Drum Set
by Ron Savage, Casey Scheuerell and the Berklee Faculty
50449429 Book/CD $14.95

Guitar
by Larry Baione and the Berklee Faculty
50449426 Book/CD $16.99

Keyboard
by Russell Hoffmann, Paul Schmeling and the Berklee Faculty
50449428 Book/CD $14.95

Viola
by Matt Glaser, Mimi Rabson and the Berklee Faculty
00101383 Book/CD $14.99

WELLNESS

MANAGE YOUR STRESS AND PAIN THROUGH MUSIC
by Dr. Suzanne B. Hanser and Dr. Susan E. Mandel
50449592 Book/CD $29.99

MUSICIAN'S YOGA
by Mia Olson
50449587 Book $14.99

THE NEW MUSIC THERAPIST'S HANDBOOK – SECOND ED.
by Dr. Suzanne B. Hanser
50449424 Book $29.95

EAR TRAINING, IMPROVISATION, MUSIC THEORY

BEGINNING EAR TRAINING
by Gilson Schachnik
50449548 Book/CD $16.99

THE BERKLEE BOOK OF JAZZ HARMONY
by Joe Mulholland & Tom Hojnacki
00113755 Book/CD $24.99

BERKLEE MUSIC THEORY – 2ND ED.
by Paul Schmeling
50449615 Rhythm, Scales Intervals: Book/CD $24.99
50449616 Harmony: Book/CD $22.99

BLUES IMPROVISATION COMPLETE
by Jeff Harrington
Book/CD Packs
50449486 B♭ Instruments $19.95
50449425 C Treble Instruments $22.99
50449487 E♭ Instruments $19.95

A GUIDE TO JAZZ IMPROVISATION
by John LaPorta
Book/CD Packs
50449439 C Instruments $19.95
50449441 B♭ Instruments $19.99
50449442 E♭ Instruments $19.99
50449443 𝄢 Instruments $19.99

IMPROVISATION FOR CLASSICAL MUSICIANS
by Eugene Friesen with Wendy M. Friesen
50449637 Book/CD $24.99

REHARMONIZATION TECHNIQUES
by Randy Felts
50449496 Book $29.95

MUSIC BUSINESS

THE FUTURE OF MUSIC
by Dave Kusek and Gerd Leonhard
50448055 Book $16.95

MAKING MUSIC MAKE MONEY
by Eric Beall
50448009 Book $26.95

MUSIC INDUSTRY FORMS
by Jonathan Feist
00121814 Book $14.99

MUSIC MARKETING
by Mike King
50449588 Book $24.99

PROJECT MANAGEMENT FOR MUSICIANS
by Jonathan Feist
50449659 Book $27.99

THE SELF-PROMOTING MUSICIAN – 3RD EDITION
by Peter Spellman
00119607 Book $24.99

MUSIC PRODUCTION & ENGINEERING

AUDIO MASTERING
by Jonathan Wyner
50449581 Book/CD $29.99

AUDIO POST PRODUCTION
by Mark Cross
50449627 Book $19.99

MIX MASTERS
by Maureen Droney
50448023 Book $24.95

PRODUCING AND MIXING HIP-HOP/R&B
by Mike Hamilton
50449555 Book/DVD-ROM $19.99

PRODUCING DRUM BEATS
by Eric Hawkins
50449598 Book/CD-ROM Pack $22.99

RECORDING AND PRODUCING IN THE HOME STUDIO
by David Franz
50448045 Book $24.95

UNDERSTANDING AUDIO
by Daniel M. Thompson
50449456 Book $24.99

SONGWRITING, COMPOSING, ARRANGING

ARRANGING FOR LARGE JAZZ ENSEMBLE
by Dick Lowell and Ken Pullig
50449528 Book/CD $39.95

COMPLETE GUIDE TO FILM SCORING – 2ND ED.
by Richard Davis
50449607 .... $27.99

JAZZ COMPOSITION
by Ted Pease
50448000 Book/CD $39.99

MELODY IN SONGWRITING
by Jack Perricone
50449419 Book/CD $24.95

MODERN JAZZ VOICINGS
by Ted Pease and Ken Pullig
50449485 Book/CD $24.95

MUSIC COMPOSITION FOR FILM AND TELEVISION
by Lalo Schifrin
50449604 Book $34.99

MUSIC NOTATION
PREPARING SCORES AND PARTS
by Matthew Nicholl and Richard Grudzinski
50449540 Book $16.99

MUSIC NOTATION
THEORY AND TECHNIQUE FOR MUSIC NOTATION
by Mark McGrain
50449399 Book $24.95

POPULAR LYRIC WRITING
by Andrea Stolpe
50449553 Book $14.95

SONGWRITING: ESSENTIAL GUIDE
by Pat Pattison
50481582 Lyric and Form Structure: Book $16.99
00124366 Rhyming: Book - 2nd Ed. . $16.99

SONGWRITING STRATEGIES
by Mark Simos
50449621 Book/CD $22.99

THE SONGWRITER'S WORKSHOP
by Jimmy Kachulis
50449519 Harmony: Book/CD $29.95
50449518 Melody: Book/CD $24.95

AUTOBIOGRAPHY

LEARNING TO LISTEN: THE JAZZ JOURNEY OF GARY BURTON
by Gary Burton
00117798 Book $27.99

HAL•LEONARD® CORPORATION
7777 W. BLUEMOUND RD. P.O. BOX 13819 MILWAUKEE, WI 53213

Prices subject to change without notice. Visit your local music dealer or bookstore, or go to www.berkleepress.com

0215